THE RETURN

Signs of the End Times and What to Expect

• • •

RICHARD ROBERTS

ISBN# 978-0-9990524-6-4

Printed in the United States of America

Signs of the End Times and What to Expect

THE RETURN

Signs of the End Times and What to Expect

by Richard Roberts

Wherever I go, people want to know about the signs of the times. They want to know about the second coming of the Lord, the Antichrist, and the cataclysmic events that will occur at the end times. They ask questions such as these:

How will the world as we know it end?

What does it mean that a new Jerusalem will come down from heaven one day?

Do I need to be concerned about the Antichrist?

How are all the end-time events described in the Bible going to happen?

How will I recognize the signs that mean Jesus will soon be coming back?

In this book, I'm going to share with you answers about the end times and the return of Jesus Christ—not to make you fearful of what is to come, but so that you may be informed. I want you to be knowledgeable of what is to come and how you can be a part of the end-time harvest, as well as understanding God's plan for His people—including you—so that you may have peace and confidence in Him in these last days.

What Jesus Taught the Disciples about the End Times

The questions many Christians are asking today about the end times were also asked by the disciples of Jesus. In fact, the Bible says that the disciples came to Jesus one day and asked about it.

MATTHEW 24:3

Now as He (Jesus) *sat on the Mount of Olives, the disciples came to Him privately, saying, "Tell us, when will these things be? And what will be the sign of Your coming, and of the end of the age?"*

Jesus answered their question by urging them to be prepared. He wasn't trying to frighten them. He simply wanted them to know what would lie ahead so that they—and we—could be ready. So He said to His disciples:

MATTHEW 24:4–8

Take heed that no one deceives you.

For many will come in My name, saying, 'I am the

Christ,' and will deceive many.

And you will hear of wars and rumors of wars. See that you are not troubled; for all these things must come to pass, but the end is not yet.

For nation will rise against nation, and kingdom against kingdom. And there will be famines, pestilences, and earthquakes in various places.

All these are the beginning of sorrows.

We are seeing many of these signs in the earth right now. These signs of the times—wars, rumors of wars, famines, pestilences, earthquakes, and other disasters—are unfolding as I write this and as you read this.

But notice what Jesus also said: "This is not yet the end." These signs are meant to capture our attention so that we can be wise, understand the times we live in, and be ready for God's plan to unfold.

Recognizing the Signs of the Times

Throughout the Church Age, believers have looked and longed for the appearing of Jesus. The Second Coming of Jesus to earth, when He will receive a glorious Church, those who believe in Him, to Himself, is a very significant event in Bible prophecy.

Because of the anxious anticipation of Jesus' return,

numerous dates for His return have been set by religious groups and various individuals. People may say they know the year and even the day that Jesus will return. But none of them have been correct, and none of this kind of date-setting will be correct in the future.

Why not? Because God Himself has already said we would not be given a date for Jesus' return, but rather a season.

First Chronicles 12:32 says that the sons of Issachar had understanding of the times, to know what Israel ought to do. This spiritual understanding of the times—the spiritual season—we live in and what to do for the Lord during that season is something that God desires us to possess. When we don't have this spiritual understanding of our times, it can be a problem. It can even cause people to miss out on recognizing who Jesus is!

That's what happened with many of the Jewish leaders of Jesus' day.

MATTHEW 16:1–3

Then the Pharisees and Sadducees came and testing Him asked that He would show them a sign from heaven.

He answered and said to them, When it is evening you say, It will be fair weather, for the sky is red;

And in the morning, It will be foul weather today, for the sky is red and threatening. Hypocrites! You know how to discern the face of the sky, but you cannot discern the signs of the times.

In Matthew 16, the Pharisees and Sadducees wanted Jesus to give them a sign as proof that He was the Messiah. These men were the religious leaders at that time. They were among the most highly educated of their society.

But despite all their education and training, these religious leaders were spiritually ignorant concerning what was happening right before their eyes. They failed to recognize the Messiah, the One for whom they were supposedly waiting. Jesus Christ, the Messiah, had no spiritual impact on their lives because they did not discern the times they were living in.

Never before in human history has civilization been more educated or more advanced than we are today. Technology is exploding all around us. Knowledge and information are more readily available today than ever before. Communication systems, transportation, and international finance have connected the earth today in ways thought impossible just a few years ago.

Yet much of society appears to be as spiritually uninformed today as they were in the days of Jesus. The fact is that many are still stumbling under the heavy load of sin and despair. People today have never been more lost and sick and in need of Jesus Christ.

Humanity's need for Jesus Christ and our responsibility as Christians to reach out to them with the Good News is one of the most important reasons why we need to understand the spiritual season we are living in. We don't need to be spiritually ignorant. The Bible can show us the truth about the signs of the times. And the Bible assures us that we can recognize the season of Jesus' second coming.

1 THESSALONIANS 5:1–6

But concerning the times and the seasons brethren, you have no need that I should write you.

For you yourselves know perfectly that the day of the Lord so comes as a thief in the night.

For when they say, "Peace and safety!" then sudden destruction comes upon them, as labor pains upon a pregnant woman. And they shall not escape.

But you, brethren, are not in darkness, so that this Day should overtake you as a thief.

You are all sons of light and sons of the day. We are not in the night nor of darkness.

Therefore let us not sleep, as others do, but let us watch and be sober.

Here, the Apostle Paul states that although we may

not know the exact time of the appearing of Jesus, we can know the season in which this prophetic event will occur. It will take place at a moment's notice, "as a thief in the night."

This sudden return might seem frightening to some—but it doesn't have to frighten us. Thanks to what the scriptures tell us, we can be ready for the Lord's return. As long as we are serving the Lord faithfully, trusting in Him and doing what He has called us to do daily, we are positioning ourselves to be prepared when He returns. And since He is coming back for us, we don't have to be afraid. Instead, we can rejoice in the knowledge that our Savior and Lord will be here soon.

I believe in my spirit that we are living in the last of the last days. Knowing this sparks tremendous hope in my heart, and it motivates me! Knowing that we are living in the season of Jesus' appearing and the catching away of the Church is motivating me and this ministry to work far harder for the Lord than ever before!

I don't feel afraid. Rather, I am excited and my faith is soaring—because I recognize the work the Lord has given me to do in this season has never been more important!

It is my prayer that you, too, will become motivated to serve Him and work for the Lord like never before until Jesus comes. I believe that if we are alert and aware of the time that we are living in, we will be ready when Jesus returns. And we can help those around us to be ready too.

The Assurance of Bible Prophecy

Whenever we want to understand God's plan for mankind and the world, we look to the Bible for our answers. The Bible contains the information we need to understand what will occur in the end times, and what is to be our part in it.

And we can have the assurance that His Word about the end times is as true as everything else the Word tells us, because over the centuries, we have seen over and over that what the Bible says, comes to pass. The prophecies given by God through His prophets over the centuries have been coming to pass. We can rest assured that Jesus will return for a glorious Church because He has promised to do so—and He keeps His Word.

Here are just a few examples of Bible prophecies coming to pass, which we can turn to as assurance that God will keep His Word to us during the end times.

- When Jesus was born of the Virgin Mary, His birth fulfilled the 700 B.C. prophecy of Isaiah 7:14, *Therefore the Lord Himself will give you a sign: Behold, the virgin shall conceive and bear a Son, and shall call his name Immanuel.*

• When Jesus launched His miracle healing ministry, it was a marvelous prophesied period of events. Jesus was arrested, crucified, rose from the grave, and then ascended into heaven to sit at the right hand of His Father—all according to prophecies given in Isaiah chapters 52, 53, and 54, and other passages throughout the Bible.

• Also, when the Holy Spirit was poured out in the Upper Room on the Day of Pentecost (Acts 2:1–4), this, too, was a prophesied event (Joel 2:28–29).

As wonderful as these prophesied events have been, there is more that God has planned for His people. He is still at work in the world today. And today, Bible prophecy is being fulfilled at an amazing rate. For those of us who are Christians, there has never been a more exciting time to be alive!

Let this thought get down on the inside of you: God is not yet finished dealing with men and women. God's plan for the earth is still unfolding, and you and I are alive and participating in the most exciting season in history. Do not miss it like the Pharisees and Sadducees did in Jesus' day. Watch and wait, and be about the Master's business as you look for His soon return.

Knowing the Season of the End Times

The Bible teaches that we are to be ready for Jesus' appearing, and also to be looking for it.

MATTHEW 24:44

Therefore you also be ready, for the Son of Man is coming at an hour you do not expect.

LUKE 21:28,36

Now when these things begin to happen, look up and lift up your heads, because your redemption draws near.

Watch therefore, and pray always that you may be counted worthy to escape all these things that will come to pass, and to stand before the Son of Man.

PHILIPPIANS 3:20–21

For our citizenship is in heaven, from which we also eagerly wait for the Savior, the Lord Jesus Christ,

Who will transform our lowly body that it may be conformed to His glorious body, according to the working by which He is able even to subdue all things to Himself.

Scriptures such as these tell us that we are to watch for Jesus' return. We are to expect it and be ready for it.

So, what are we looking for? What are the signs that

His return is drawing closer? Jesus Himself gave us some instruction on how to recognize the season we are living in—signs that would signal the end times are near. Let's look more closely at the passage we read earlier.

> MATTHEW 24:4–8
> *Take heed that no one deceives you.*
> *For many will come in My name, saying, 'I am the Christ,' and will deceive many.*
> *And you will hear of wars and rumors of wars. See that you are not troubled; for all these things must come to pass, but the end is not yet.*
> *For nation will rise against nation, and kingdom against kingdom. And there will be famines, pestilences, and earthquakes in various places.*
> *All these are the beginning of sorrows.*

According to Jesus, one of the key signs that the end times are approaching is that there will be wars and rumors of wars, and nation rising up against nation. All we need to do is turn on the news to see that this is happening right now. There is unrest in many parts of the world. There are civil wars happening within some nations, and there are border wars and rumors of possible wars between nations.

Another thing that will happen as the end times draw

near is a rise in false prophets—people who claim to be speaking for God but who, in reality, say things that go against the Word of God. Today, the world is full of such voices.

And there will also be signs that the natural order of things is being disrupted. There will be an increase in pestilences—diseases that are fatal and hard to prevent, new forms of sickness we've never seen before, and epidemics that harm many people. There's going to be famine. There will be an increase in earthquakes and other natural disasters. We're seeing all of this right now.

Let me give you just one example of how the natural world is going through an upheaval.

I grew up in Oklahoma. When I was a boy, we never heard of earthquakes happening in our state. But now, Oklahoma is experiencing earthquakes all the time. They're small earthquakes, but they're still happening—and they're happening in places where they have never happened before.

Changes like these in the natural order are becoming more and more common all over the world. But remember what Jesus said. "All these things must happen, but this is not yet the end." There are still many things that will take place before Jesus returns.

The Parable of the Fig Tree

Now, let's look closely at something else Jesus said that can help us recognize the signs of the times.

LUKE 21:29–33

Then He (Jesus) *spoke to them a parable: Look at the fig tree, and all the trees.*

When they are already budding, you see and know for yourselves that summer is now near.

So you also, when you see these things happening, know that the kingdom of God is near.

Assuredly, I say to you, this generation will by no means pass away till all things take place.

Heaven and earth will pass away, but My words will by no means pass away.

In this passage, Jesus discusses the fig tree and all the other trees. Now, when Jesus was talking about the fig tree, He wasn't just talking about a natural plant. He also was conveying a spiritual message, because throughout the Bible, God used the fig tree as a biblical symbol of Israel. When the Bible speaks of the fig tree, it is speaking about the nation of Israel.

If the fig tree represents the nation of Israel, then the other trees Jesus spoke about must represent other nations. In this passage of Luke, Jesus is saying that we can look to Israel and the nations of the world for more evidence that we are in the season of His appearing.

Today, the actions of many nations point to the fulfillment of prophecy in Scripture. And it all has to do with what is happening today in the tiny nation in the Middle East known as Israel.

Remember—God's plan to redeem man from the power of sin began in the Garden of Eden, when He promised to send a Savior. To bring about the birth of that Savior and to ensure that His promises were preserved for future generations, God established a covenant with a man named Abraham. Abraham's seed, his children—the nation of Israel—was promised and eventually formed.

In the fullness of God's timing, Jesus was born into the world. He lived a sinless life, died for us on the cross, and was resurrected as our glorious Lord and Savior. Not long after Jesus was crucified, the Roman Empire destroyed Jerusalem.

But God was not done with the nation of Israel yet. He waited for just the right time to restore Israel, a miracle promised in the Scriptures. For the restoration of the land of Israel was to be one sign that the end times were drawing near. And if you know your history, you know the rebirth of Israel finally happened on May 14,

1948. That's when Israel was allowed to function again as a nation.

On the same day, May 14, 1948, the combined Arab world declared war on the tiny nation of Israel, which was not even one day old. And the hostilities between Israel and the Arab world continue up to this present day.

The truth is, though, that this hostility between Israel and its neighbors isn't new. It is an age-old feud that started when Abraham had two sons—Isaac, the son God promised he would have through his wife Sarah, and Ishmael, the son born of Abraham's fear and frustration, through Sarah's handmaiden, Hagar.

The Israelis and the Arabs are blood kin. Both of them are descendants of Abraham. The Jewish race, the Israelis, came through Isaac and Jacob. Most Arab races came through Ishmael. Ever since the birth of these two family lines, there has been a 4,000-year-old family feud over land. And the rebirth of this conflict in the Middle East is another sign of the end times.

Israel and the Nations of the World

In Luke 21, when Jesus said, "Consider the fig tree and all the trees," He was confirming other nations would appear on the scene with Israel in the end times. In fact, the United States of America, became involved in the fulfillment of this scripture. This happened in 1948, when President Harry Truman agreed to support the formation of the nation of Israel.

At that moment in time, the United States began a major prophetic assignment by becoming a sponsor of the nation of Israel. This role, for as long as the support of Israel continues, brings the U.S. under the canopy of God's Abrahamic blessing.

GENESIS 12:1–3

Get out of your country, from your family and from your father's house, to a land that I will show you.

I will make you a great nation; I will bless you and make your name great; and you shall be a blessing.

I will bless those who bless you, and I will curse him who curses you; and in you all the families of the earth shall be blessed.

Why do you think we in the United States have been a prosperous and blessed nation? The Lord has taken me around the world ministering to people far and wide. I assure you there is no place like America. We are truly blessed of the Lord. Make no mistake about it—the U.S. is one of the most blessed nations on earth because, for the most part, we have blessed the nation of Israel.

I do not mean the U.S. is perfect. We have our problems. But the hand of God has been upon us. And it is terribly important that the United States stay focused and continue its support of God's chosen, Israel—lest we find ourselves on the other side of the blessing, *"I will curse him who curses you."*

The Good News Will Be Preached to All People

Another common question that I've been asked is, "Richard, what do you mean when you talk about an end-time transfer of wealth? What do finances have to do with the return of Jesus?"

Well, friend, it takes finances to share the Gospel around the world! And that's what the end-time transfer of wealth is all about.

PROVERBS 13:22

A good man leaves an inheritance to his children's children,

But the wealth of the sinner is stored up for the righteous.

I want you to look at the second half of that verse. It says the wealth of the sinner is stored up for the righteous. Resources will come from the hands of the unrighteous, from the wicked, from the world, and they will be transferred over into the hands of the righteous.

Who are the righteous? The righteous are Christian believers. And what is the purpose of that transfer of wealth? Is it so that Christians can become wealthy? No! That's not the purpose of the end-time transfer of wealth.

Friend, the purpose of transferring the wealth of the wicked into the hands of the righteous is so that we can use those resources for the work of God. It's so that we can give to the spreading of the Gospel around the world. It is for the end-time harvest of souls.

JOHN 3:16–17

For God so loved the world that He gave His only begotten Son, that whoever believes in Him should not perish but have everlasting life.

For God did not send His Son into the world to condemn the world, but that the world through Him might be saved.

1 THESSALONIANS 4:17–18

Then we who are alive and remain shall be caught up together with them in the clouds to meet the Lord in the air. And thus we shall always be with the Lord.

Therefore comfort one another with these words.

Everything God does in the earth is about bringing people back into fellowship with Him. This is the reason that Jesus came the first time (John 3:16–17). And when He comes the second time, He will be coming for His own (1 Thessalonians 4:17–18). The Lord God Almighty is going to reveal Himself to everyone on the face of the earth.

But before His return, the Bible tells us that all people will have the opportunity to hear the Gospel.

MATTHEW 24:14

And this gospel of the kingdom will be preached in all the world as a witness to all the nations, and then the end will come.

How is this scripture going to come to pass? How will the end-time harvest of souls take place? It's going to happen through Christians who use the wealth of the wicked to go to the nations of the earth with the Gospel of Jesus Christ. I mean, every tribe, every tongue, every people group, every nationality, every ethnic group—everyone on earth will have an opportunity to make a choice between heaven and hell.

Now, there are people in the world today who don't believe that there is a literal hell, but I have news. It doesn't matter what they believe. There is a heaven to gain and there is a hell to shun. Hell is not just a swear word. Hell is a place, and, believe me, you don't want to go there. Hell was not created for people. It was created for the devil and all of the angels who were kicked out of Heaven with him.

I also realize that there are people in hell today, but that was not God's plan. There are people who reject God totally, and that's how a person goes to hell. They reject God totally and, when they die, they go to hell, where they are separated from God for eternity.

This is why it matters so much for us to share the Gospel around the world. We must share the saving, healing, delivering, restoring message of Jesus with everyone we can reach. And when the message has been shared with all peoples everywhere, then—and only then—can the end come.

The Rapture of the Church

Once everyone on earth has heard the Word of God and has had an opportunity to surrender their life to God, the next thing that will happen is a cataclysmic event called the Rapture.

1 THESSALONIANS 4:13–18

But I do not want you to be ignorant, brethren,

concerning those who have fallen asleep, lest you sorrow as others who have no hope.

For if we believe that Jesus died and rose again, even so God will bring with Him those who sleep in Jesus.

For this we say to you by the word of the Lord, that we who are alive and remain until the coming of the Lord will by no means precede those who are asleep.

For the Lord Himself will descend from heaven with a shout, with the voice of an archangel, and with the trumpet of God. And the dead in Christ will rise first.

Then we who are alive and remain shall be caught up together with them in the clouds to meet the Lord in the air. And thus we shall always be with the Lord.

Therefore comfort one another with these words.

According to 1 Thessalonians, there is coming a day when the Lord Himself will come down from heaven with a shout. And the voice of an archangel and the trumpet of God will sound, and the Lord's voice from heaven will say, "Come up here." And there will be a catching away of God's people to heaven. That's what the word rapture means—it's a "catching away."

Now, I know that there are some who do not believe in a literal Rapture. But 1 Thessalonians 4 makes it clear that there will be a literal catching away, or Rapture, of the body of Christ – those who are Christians. Make no mistake about it. There will be a literal Rapture.

You may say, "Richard, what's going to happen when the Rapture takes place?"

The first thing that will happen is that the Christians who have died in the faith, every Christian who has died before us, will be taken up from their graves. You may say, "But their bodies are dead. They're decomposed. They're just bones. And what about those who have been cremated or lost at sea?" None of that matters, because God is going to restore them. They will be given new bodies, and they will go to heaven. They will go first.

Then the Christians who are still alive at the time of the Rapture will be caught up to meet the Lord in the air. And I'm talking about perhaps a billion or more Christians on this earth will suddenly be gone.

Two workers will be sitting at desks, and one will suddenly be gone, while the other will suddenly be sitting there wondering where they went. That's what's going to happen. In the twinkling of an eye, it will happen. All the Christians on earth will be gone. When this happens, the world will not know what hit them. There will be chaos.

Why Does the Rapture Need to Take Place?

The answer is given by Jesus in Matthew 24.

MATTHEW 24:37–39

But as the days of Noah were, so also will the coming of the Son of Man be.

For as in the days before the flood, they were eating and drinking, marrying and giving in marriage, until the day that Noah entered the ark,

And did not know until the flood came and took them all away, so also will the coming of the Son of Man be.

Before destruction comes, God always removes the righteous remnant. If you go back through history, when God was about to destroy the world through a flood in Noah's day, what did He do? He removed Noah and his family, the only righteous family on earth at that time. Before He caused a rain for 40 days and 40 nights that flooded the world, He forewarned Noah and led him to build an ark so that he and his family, who were the only God believing people on earth at that time, might be saved. God also told Noah to take along two each of the animals that were on the earth, to preserve them from the destruction that was about to take place.

A similar thing happened with Sodom and Gomorrah. Before those two cities were destroyed for their immoral lifestyle, God removed the righteous. Lot, his wife, and family were brought safely out of the cities so they could escape the destruction that was soon to happen.

And God will do exactly the same thing before the final part of the end times. Before those evil days come to pass, God will remove the righteous remnant. When the Rapture happens, the whole world will seem to go dark, and there will be no one left on earth but the unrighteous. There will be no one left on earth but those who have rejected Christ and salvation, and that's when the Antichrist will rise.

The Coming of the Antichrist

Now, another common question that people ask is, "Who is the Antichrist? Is the Antichrist alive? Is he in the world now?"

I don't know the answers to those questions, but I do know this. The Bible says that the power that has restrained the Antichrist has been the Church, the body of Christ, believers—and the Holy Spirit at work in us to display the power and love of Jesus Christ. That's what has been holding the devil and the Antichrist back.

2 THESSALONIANS 2:7–8

For the mystery of lawlessness is already at work; only He who now restrains will do so until He is taken out of the way.

And then the lawless one will be revealed…

The devil cannot release the Antichrist into the world, and his identity will not be known, until the Rapture occurs. Imagine what will happen on earth when all the Christians, all their prayers, all their obedient actions in the service of God, and all their anointed, Holy Spirit-led ministries vanish from the earth! There will be a huge vacuum of power.

And that will be when Satan moves in. That is when he will reveal the identity of the Antichrist. The Antichrist will then begin to set up his kingdom. This will take place only after we Christians are caught away to be safely with the Lord.

A lot of people today have been concerned and worried about the Antichrist. Many are terrified of just the thought of him. But the Bible tells us there is no need whatsoever for us to be afraid. You don't need to be terrified of the Antichrist because the Holy Spirit is restraining him. Christians on this earth and their prayers are restraining him. And he will not come into his true power until we are gone.

"But, Richard," you may say, "is the Antichrist living on earth right now?" Now, there are many theologians who believe that the Antichrist is alive today. On the other hand, there are many who believe he has not yet been born. The truth is, nobody knows. You can make all the suppositions you want, but even Jesus Himself doesn't know the details of God's timing for end-time events. The Bible says only the Father knows the days and times when these events will take place (Matthew 24:36).

In other words, we know a lot about the Antichrist from what the Bible tells us, but we don't know exactly when he will make his appearance. Here's what we do know, according to what the Scriptures tell us.

According to the Bible, the Antichrist will be a charismatic world leader who will come onto the world stage at a time when there is great chaos. The Bible indicates that he will come out of the former Greco-Roman world, which means he will most likely be a European, probably from the southern area of Europe. He will command Europe, and he will try to command the whole world. He'll be a man of great cunning and great intelligence, and he will seemingly solve many of the world's problems (Daniel 8:23–25).

The Bible calls him the son of perdition and the son of satan. He will be a liar and a master deceiver. He will be a liar. But let me say it again to reassure you—the

Bible says that the Antichrist cannot and will not be revealed until after the Rapture of the Church. We, who are Christians, will not be here when he appears.

When the Antichrist arises, the world will be undergoing some great cataclysm—partly due to the chaos of the Rapture, and possibly due to the natural disasters, wars, and pestilences that Matthew 24 tells us will happen before the end comes. Because of the chaos, people will be terrified, and they will be looking for a leader to save them. This is when the Antichrist will quickly rise and take his seat of authority.

The Antichrist will gather all his forces, taking in more and more territory. And there will begin a seven year period called the Great Tribulation. Much of the Book of Revelation covers this period—and the body of Christ will not physically be on earth when it happens. We will see the events from heaven, where we have been caught up to be safely with the Lord while these events take place on earth.

The First Half of the Tribulation

The Book of Revelation indicates that the events of the Tribulation will be divided in half. The first three and a half years of this Tribulation period will seem to be peaceful at first to many people, because the Antichrist will come on the scene with seemingly great wisdom. He will appear to solve world problems in the blink of an eye, and people will begin to look to him as if he is a god.

The Antichrist will most likely set up his kingdom in Rome. And he will quickly rise in power, hoping to dominate the whole world. He'll build a great army, and he will begin conquering the world. He'll be responsible for nuclear war. His first war will take out one third of the population of the whole world.

During this period, the plagues spoken of in the Book of Revelation and the Book of Daniel will begin to happen. There will be such plagues as the world has never seen, producing much torment and suffering on the earth.

The Antichrist Is Mortally Wounded—Then Restored to Life

One of the most dramatic events of the Tribulation will be what appears to be a miracle. In truth, it won't be a miracle; like everything the devil does, it will be a mockery of God and a perversion. But to the world, it will appear as a miracle to deceive many.

REVELATION 13:3

And I saw one of his heads as if it had been mortally wounded, and his deadly wound was healed. And all the world marveled and followed the beast.

At the halfway point of the Tribulation, the Antichrist will be mortally wounded. This will happen after the Antichrist breaks a peace treaty he has made with Israel. There will be an assassination attempt on his life. Some theologians believe that he will be killed and then be restored to life by demonic power.

Others believe that he will appear to be dead and that he will appear to have risen from the dead. I believe this will be the case, because only God has resurrection power, and it would not be consistent with His nature to resurrect this ungodly man.

I personally believe that what will happen will be a situation in mockery of what happened to the Apostle Paul when he was stoned for preaching in a certain city, and they dragged his body outside the city, thinking that he was dead. He appeared to be dead to them, but he wasn't dead. He was unconscious. The disciples gathered around and prayed, and Paul regained consciousness and was restored to his ministry. I personally believe that's what will happen when the Antichrist appears to come back from the dead.

But however it happens, there will be an attempt to assassinate the Antichrist. He will appear to have a mortal, deadly wound. Yet he will rise up from that wound. That's when the devil will specifically come inside him and possess him fully. At this point, all hell will be released. The Antichrist will begin his reign of terror in the last three and a half years of the Tribulation.

The Unholy Trinity

Now, when the Antichrist takes power after his recovery from his mortal wound, he will have a three-tiered leadership, just like God does. Through Satan, who empowers him, there will be an imitation of the Holy Trinity of God—Father, Son and Holy Spirit. But because the devil only does evil, this will be a terrible, unholy trinity——really, a mockery of God and all things holy.

Understanding the Holy Trinity helps us to understand what the Book of Revelation tells us about the Antichrist's rulership. You see, in the spirit realm, there is God the Father; Jesus, His Son, who He empowers; and the Holy Spirit, who honors Jesus.

During the end times, Satan will set up a like kingdom in his own satanic way, with Satan acting as a false god; and the Antichrist being like his son, whom he empowers; and then there'll be a false prophet acting as a false Holy Spirit.

The False Prophet

Many Christians have asked, "Who will this false prophet be?" And there are many theories people put forth as to who this false prophet will be. But just as with the Antichrist, we don't yet know who the false prophet is. We do not know if he is alive in the world now or not. But we can know what the Bible tells us about him.

According to the Scriptures, the Antichrist will have a human accomplice who will have the demonic calling of deceiving the nations "religiously." His goal will be to draw the world's worship to the image of the Beast—the Antichrist. He will appear as a legitimate spiritual leader but will speak things that are opposed to the Word of God.

Revelation 13:11–15

Then I saw another beast coming up out of the earth, and he had two horns like a lamb and spoke like a dragon.

And he exercises all the authority of the first beast in his presence, and causes the earth and those who dwell in it to worship the first beast, whose deadly wound was healed.

He performs great signs, so that he even makes fire come down from heaven on the earth in the sight of men.

And he deceives those who dwell on the earth by those

signs which he was granted to do in the sight of the beast, telling those who dwell on the earth to make an image to the beast who was wounded by the sword and lived.

He was granted power to give breath to the image of the beast, that the image of the beast should both speak and cause as many as would not worship the image of the beast to be killed.

Because it will appear as if the Antichrist has been miraculously brought back from death, many people will treat him as if he is a god. And the False Prophet will have the ability to bring great deception in this time, causing many on the earth to worship the Antichrist. I believe that he will be able to do this because of cunning occult powers. Consider what the Apostle Paul says concerning the Antichrist's operation:

2 THESSALONIANS 2:9

The coming of the lawless one is according to the working of Satan, with all power, signs, and lying wonders…

What are lying wonders? I believe they will be clever maneuvers designed to appear as genuine miracles in an attempt to deceive all mankind. However, I do not believe that the works of either the Antichrist or the False Prophet will be true miracles. They will appear to be miraculous, but they will not be genuine.

The False Prophet will use his influence and these seeming miracles to lead people astray. He will create an image of the Beast, the Antichrist, and then threaten to kill everyone who will not worship the Antichrist. The worship of the image will introduce idolatry, which God has always rejected.

The Abomination of Desolation

As the second half of the Tribulation takes place, a terrible event that also mocks God will take place in Jerusalem. The Antichrist will march into the temple in Jerusalem, which will have been rebuilt by then, and he will commit what the Bible calls the abomination of desolation. In a total mockery of the Lord, he will go into the rebuilt temple in Jerusalem and declare himself to be God.

2 THESSALONIANS 2:3–4

Let no one deceive you by any means; for that Day will not come unless the falling away comes first, and the man of sin is revealed, the son of perdition,

Who opposes and exalts himself above all that is called God or that is worshipped, so that he sits as God in the temple of God, showing himself that he is God.

At this point, the Jews will recognize that they have been wrong about the true identity of Jesus Christ. They will realize He was their promised Messiah. And to escape the wrath of the Antichrist, they will flee. Many will be killed.

Others will escape to the hills and desert areas outside of Jerusalem. And there, they will find Bibles. I know this will happen because many years ago, back in the 1950s when I was a boy, our ministry took part in putting thousands and thousands of Bibles in cases in the caves and mountains in the deserts outside Jerusalem. They will be found, and they will be read.

Millions of Jews will become Christians and come to the Lord during this terrible period. And the Lord will protect them from the forces of the Antichrist.

Out of that group of Jewish people, God will raise up 144,000 Jewish evangelists who will circle the globe to share the truth of Jesus Christ. Many people will get saved during the Tribulation. Many who did not believe God before will give their hearts to Christ. And they will be martyred, but they will go to heaven because they believe on Jesus.

Those who do not receive the Gospel will go in the other direction. They will begin to say, "Great is our god, the Antichrist."

REVELATION 13:4

So they worshiped the dragon who gave authority to the beast; and they worshiped the beast, saying, Who is like the beast? Who is able to make war with him?

REVELATION 13:8–9

All who dwell on the earth will worship him, whose names have not been written in the Book of Life of the Lamb slain from the foundation of the world.

If anyone has an ear, let him hear.

Those who do not turn to God during this time will begin to worship the Beast, the Antichrist.

The True Nature of the Antichrist

The true nature of the Antichrist will not become apparent to the world until the second half of the Tribulation Period. During the first half, he will pass himself off as a peacemaker. He will appear to be an excellent leader, a very accomplished diplomat. He will successfully combine the governments, commerce, military, and religions of ten nations. Through these successes, he will create the system of the Beast, a government that he is the head of.

At the mid-point of the Tribulation, he will begin

his attempt to conquer the world as a dictator. It will be clear that he is not a man of peace. And it will also be clear that he hates God.

REVELATION 13:6

Then he opened his mouth in blasphemy against God, to blaspheme His name, His tabernacle, and those who dwell in heaven.

The Antichrist will blaspheme the many people who have escaped him and his system. He will make war against any who serve God during this time. And his power will come from the devil himself.

REVELATION 13:2

...The dragon gave him his power, his throne, and great authority.

The Antichrist will have satanic power and authority to make war against the 144,000 Jewish evangelists, their converts, and the hidden remnant of Israel. But he will not be successful! Why? Because Satan's power and authority pales in comparison to God's power and authority!

The Mark of the Beast

Back in the early 1970s, it was believed by many that the mark of the beast was already here and that it could be found in the barcodes at supermarkets and on clothing tags at every retailer. This is a common misconception; it's not true.

That's right; I said it's not true. There is no mark of the beast on anything in the world today. In the Book of Revelation, the mark of the beast is not introduced until the middle of the Tribulation Period by the False Prophet. By that time, the Church will have already been in heaven for three and a half years.

Many people ask me, "But, Richard, what about all the technologies that are available today? What about all the talk about putting a chip in the back of your hand so you can buy and sell things? What about the Internet and what it can do?"

Friend, all these new discoveries and advancements and technologies are not bad. They are not evil in and of themselves. They exist to help mankind right now, and when they are used by people who are righteous, they can be used for good. But when the Church, the body of Christ, is gone from the earth after the Rapture, Satan will then take those technologies, pervert them, and use them for his own power.

As the second half of the Tribulation progresses, the situation on earth will become increasingly more critical. There will be less commerce and trade happening, because there will be very little left to buy or sell due to famine and wars. Through the mark of the beast, the Antichrist will attempt to take over as much of the world's remaining commercial operations as possible.

To be able to buy and sell anything, people will have to take the mark on either their right hand or forehead. The Antichrist and his government will use the mark and the threat of death to coerce people to surrender to him and serve him as God.

REVELATION 13:16–18

He causes all, both small and great, rich and poor, free and slave, to receive a mark on their right hand or on their foreheads,

And that no one may buy or sell except one who has the mark or the name of the beast, or the number of his name.

Here is wisdom. Let him who has understanding calculate the number of the beast, for it is the number of a man: his number is 666.

You may be asking, "Richard, what exactly is the mark of the beast? What does it mean to take the mark?" It is a mark of willing obedience to the Antichrist. It isn't something that people will take by accident, or use unknowingly.

During this time, the Antichrist will demand to be worshiped like a god, and he will require people on earth to take his mark. Those who do so will know exactly what they are doing. This is why people who choose to take the mark are doomed to hell—they are choosing the Antichrist as their god.

But what does the number itself mean? Why 666? Biblical scholars tell us that the number six represents man. The number six also indicates incompleteness. Therefore, the number of the Beast is incomplete times three, and it will ultimately fail. The Antichrist's government will be very destructive in its season, but it will also be imperfect. And it will end.

Revelation 14:9–11

Then a third angel followed them, saying with a loud voice, if anyone worships the beast and his image, and receives his mark on his forehead or on his hand,

He himself shall also drink of the wine of the wrath of God, which is poured out full strength into the cup of His indignation. He shall be tormented with fire and brimstone in the presence of the holy angels and in the presence of the Lamb.

And the smoke of their torment ascends forever and ever;

and they have no rest day or night, who worship the beast and his image, and whoever receives the mark of his name.

The Season of the Harlot

We have already discussed the abundance of false worship and deception that the Antichrist and False Prophet will introduce during the Tribulation Period. But the Book of Revelation reveals another satanic system which started centuries ago that will feed into the season of the Antichrist. The Bible calls this system Babylon, the harlot.

REVELATION 17:4–5

The woman was arrayed in purple and scarlet, and adorned with gold and precious stones and pearls, having in her hand a golden cup full of abominations and the filthiness of her fornication.

And on her forehead a name was written: MYSTERY, BABYLON THE GREAT, THE MOTHER OF HARLOTS AND OF THE ABOMINATIONS OF THE EARTH.

Put simply, the harlot personifies every false religion that has existed since mankind's fall in the Garden of Eden. In the end times, the harlot, Babylon, will be a combination of all mankind's false religions into one organization. And this false religion will deceive millions with its false powers.

This falling away from God and pursuit of false religions was talked about by the Apostle Paul.

1 TIMOTHY 4:1–3

Now the Spirit expressly says that in the latter times some will depart from the faith, giving heed to deceiving spirits and doctrines of demons,

Speaking lies in hypocrisy, having their own conscience seared with a hot iron,

Forbidding to marry, and commanding to abstain from foods which God created to be received with thanksgiving by those who believe and know the truth.

You might be asking, "But how is the harlot operating today?" Just stop and consider the various false religions we see today. They are all operating under the influence of the devil and his attempts to deceive and lead people astray.

It's important to note that the harlot is not meant to represent any single religion or religious denomination. Rather, she represents all the religions that man has invented over the course of human history.

This spiritual deception will reach its height during the Tribulation. Many people will be deceived into thinking that the Antichrist is the Messiah. And for a time, the harlot—this false religion—will rule in harmony with the Antichrist. During this time, the Antichrist will use the false religions represented by the harlot to gather more power.

But the Bible says that the time will come when Satan will demand the world's worship of only one false god...the Devil himself. And he will destroy the harlot in order to divert all worship to himself.

Armageddon

During the Tribulation, there will be plagues and terrible suffering like we have never seen before. There will be terrible wars too. But the most dramatic of them will surely be the battle at the Valley of Megiddo, which is what people call Armageddon. At this time, a 200 million man army will rise up to come against the Antichrist and his kingdom, to resist being taken over by his world dictatorship. They will march on the Valley of Megiddo.

At that time, the sun will become black and the moon will be turned red as blood. These two phenomena will occur on the final day of the Tribulation.

MATTHEW 24:29

Immediately after the tribulation of those days the sun will be darkened, and the moon will not give its light…

REVELATION 6:12

I looked when he opened the sixth seal, and behold, there was a great earthquake; and the sun become black as sackcloth of hair, and the moon became like blood.

ZECHARIAH 14:6–7

It shall come to pass in that day that there will be no light; the lights will diminish.

It shall be one day which is known to the Lord—neither day nor night. But at evening time it shall happen that it will be light.

Around this time, there will be a brief time period where there will be no light from the sun, moon, or stars. Revelation 16:10 clarifies that natural light will be withheld from the Throne of the Beast, meaning the geographic region over which the Antichrist is ruling at the time of these events.

At this time, Jesus will return in all His glory. Every eye on this earth will see Him. The Bible says that fire will come from Jesus' mouth. It will be like a nuclear blast, and the 200 million man army will be destroyed in the flash of a second.

A great earthquake will divide the Mount of Olives to make a port out of the city of Jerusalem. Waters will flow from the Mediterranean Sea to the Dead Sea. The Lord will stand on the Mount of Olives, and He will speak the Word out of His mouth like a two-edged sword to destroy the 200 million man army.

Those gathered against the Lord will be immediately stricken blind as their eyes are consumed away in their sockets, and dumb as their tongues are consumed away in their mouths. In fright, they will reach out and grab one another and will frighten each other all the more. Ultimately, they will turn and fight among themselves with their flesh falling away from their bones and their blood gushing to the earth, creating an immense pool of blood described in Revelation 14:20. The blood will cover an area of about 185 square miles. The Bible says that the blood in the Valley of Megiddo will rise as high as the bridles of horses that day.

HEBREWS 9:28

So Christ was offered once to bear the sins of many. To those who eagerly wait for Him He will appear a second time, apart from sin, for salvation.

The Second Coming of Jesus Christ to earth will

come to pass only after He appears to receive the Church unto Himself during the Rapture, and after the Tribulation Period has been fully completed.

When Jesus returns the second time, He will deal with sin, but not in the way He dealt with it the first time. The first time Jesus came to earth, He bore the sins of many. The second time, Jesus will destroy Satan's followers who have rejected His sacrifice.

At this point, the Battle of Armageddon will already be over. The Antichrist and the False Prophet will be captured, and they'll be thrown into the lake of fire. An archangel will chain up the devil and cast him into the abyss, into the pit for a thousand years. Those who have been part of the system of the Antichrist will be destroyed. Satan will be bound for 1,000 years. And Jesus will take over the governments of the world as He begins His 1,000 year reign!

When Jesus returns to earth, you and I who are in heaven will come down with Him, along with all of the saints. We will begin our millennial 1,000-year reign upon this earth.

REVELATION 20:4

And I saw thrones, and they sat on them, and judgment was committed to them…

While in heaven around the throne, you and I will receive our assignments for future duties during the Millennium. Then we will return with Jesus to administer His kingdom on earth. There will be a theocratic government system established that will operate with perfect harmony. Every position of authority, from the local level to the highest governmental official, will be filled by the saints who have returned with Jesus.

The Millennium will be an era of health and peace. Obviously, because Satan will be bound during this period, he will not have the ability to influence what God is doing on the earth during this time period.

During the Millennium, God will continue to reach out with mercy to the survivors of the Tribulation who did not bow to the Antichrist. God will give all men and women every opportunity to receive Jesus during this period of His mercy, waiting until after the Millennium to judge the wicked. Many nations will be saved during the Millennium (Revelation 21:24).

The Final Judgment

At the end of the Millennium, all the wicked dead from the time of Adam until the end of the Millennium will be resurrected to be judged by God at the Great White Throne Judgment.

REVELATION 20:5–6

But the rest of the dead did not live again until the thousand years were finished. This is the first resurrection.

Blessed and holy is he who has part in the first resurrection. Over such the second death has no power, but they shall be priests of God and of Christ, and shall reign with Him a thousand years.

The first resurrection refers to those of us who served Christ before the Lord returns to earth, whether raptured or converted to Christianity after the Tribulation begins. We will all enjoy the millennial reign of Christ. After that period is over, there will be a brief period during which Satan is released from his imprisonment. Every person who does not accept Jesus as Savior and Lord will have an opportunity to follow Satan when he is released from the bottomless pit at the end of the 1,000-year period.

It is shocking that sin will still carry the power to resist and reject God's mercy and grace during Christ's physical and visible kingdom. But it will happen.

Once Satan is released, he will go about the earth in one last attempt to deceive as many as possible. He will gather a large following of people and will lead them against the saints and the Holy City. God will send fire from heaven to end this battle so swiftly, it will be as though the battle never occurred. Satan will again be taken captive and cast into the lake of fire, where he will be tormented for eternity.

The only people left alive on the earth after this event will be the believers from all time periods, the righteous remnant of Israel, and the nations saved during Christ's reign, who will populate the new earth.

REVELATION 20:7–15

Now when the thousand years have expired, Satan will be released from his prison

And will go out to deceive the nations which are in the four corners of the earth, Gog and Magog, to gather them together to battle, whose number is as the sand of the sea.

They went up on the breadth of the earth and surrounded the camp of the saints and the beloved city. And fire came down from God out of heaven and devoured them.

The devil, who deceived them, was cast into the lake of fire and brimstone where the beast and the false prophet are. And they will be tormented day and night forever and ever.

Then I saw a great white throne and Him who sat on it, from whose face the earth and the heaven fled away. And there was found no place for them.

And I saw the dead, small and great, standing before God, and books were opened. And another book was opened, which is the Book of Life. And the dead were judged according to their works, by the things which were written in the books.

The sea gave up the dead who were in it, and Death and Hades delivered up the dead who were in them. And they were judged, each one according to his works.

Then Death and Hades were cast into the lake of fire. This is the second death.

And anyone not found written in the Book of Life was cast into the lake of fire.

The wicked dead of all ages will be resurrected to stand before God's throne in this final resurrection at the end of the Millennium. No one will be left on earth, and hell will be emptied. Those there to be judged will include all nations which did not turn to God before and after the Tribulation, and the fallen angels referred to in Jude 6.

A New Heaven and a New Earth

Revelation 21:1–2

Now I saw a new heaven and a new earth, for the first heaven and the first earth had passed away. Also there was no more sea.

Then I, John, saw the holy city, New Jerusalem,

coming down out of heaven from God, prepared as a bride adorned for her husband.

Combined together on the new earth will be all the righteous people saved during the Tribulation and the Millennium, the nation of Israel fully restored during the Millennium, the Church, the Old Testament saints, the 144,000 Jewish evangelists, and the Two Witnesses. All will have glorified bodies. We will live in the New Jerusalem and continue serving as administrators of Jesus' everlasting kingdom.

A Glorious Church—Not a Fearful Church

You and I are living as a part of a marked generation! We could have been born thousands of years ago, which would have prevented us from being part of today's last-days events. But no, you and I are here to witness the greatest hour of the fulfillment of Bible prophecy. This is the greatest hour to be alive!

There are no Bible days of the past that can even begin to compare with these days. Let's be sure that we are making the most of them!

How do we do that? We do it by fulfilling God's Word. Remember, the Lord will return to receive unto

Himself a glorious Church. You and I, as Christians, are a part of that glorious Church. So, let's talk for a moment about what we—"the glorious Church"—should be like.

I believe we should be moving forward on all fronts! We should be meeting the devil head on and not falling for his tricks and strategies. We should not sit idly by while sin, sickness, disease, and lack of every kind ruin the lives of those around us.

A glorious Church is you and me standing up and taking the healing ministry of Jesus Christ to a crying, sighing, dying world. A glorious Church is you and me ministering under a mighty anointing of the Holy Spirit, bringing deliverance to people desperately in need.

A glorious Church is you and me being faithful and obedient unto the Lord so we can continue to walk in His anointing and accomplish His will for our lives—reaping the harvest fields in every corner of the globe!

MATTHEW 16:18

On this rock I will build My Church, and the gates of hell shall not prevail against it.

If you want to know why I believe we have no need to fear the end times, here is one reason. We are the end-time Church! As Christians, our lives are built on the foundation of the Word of God. The gates of hell can't prevail against it.

Yes, this world is becoming darker as the end draws nearer. But the darker it gets, the brighter God's light will shine forth through us! Friend, fear and dread should be the farthest things from our minds. Instead, we should be looking to the harvest fields and seeing who we can draw to Christ before the Tribulation begins.

The Greatest Love Story of All

When Jesus was crucified, they took His lifeless body down and put Him in the grave. He was in there for three days. What was He doing? The Bible says He went down into the upper part of hell, called paradise, and He took captivity captive. Now, what does that mean? That means He rescued the righteous souls, those who had died in faith, those who had died waiting on the Lord, and He took them directly to heaven. (Ephesians 4:8-10).

Then Jesus came back and showed Himself alive to hundreds on this earth. He said, "I'm ascending to My Father, but I will come again." When this Gospel of the kingdom is preached to all people, all nations, all tribes, all tongues, and everyone in the world has an opportunity to hear the Gospel of Jesus, then will begin the Second Coming of the Lord.

You talk about a great love story! It's not doom and

gloom. No, it's the greatest love story of all. He loves you so much. He wants you to know that love, and He wants everyone in this world to know that love too.

Jesus said, "You shall be witnesses unto Me in Jerusalem, Judea, Samaria and to the uttermost parts of the earth." We are to be witnesses in our homes, witnesses in our families, witnesses in our communities, witnesses in our jobs, witnesses in places where it's difficult, all to help usher in the Second Coming of the Lord.

The Gospel of Jesus Christ must be preached as a witness to all people groups, all nations, all over the world. Why must we share this message? Here's why.

Jesus went to the cross and shed His own blood for the forgiveness of sin. He took the stripes on his back, so that you and I might be healed in every area of our lives. He made Himself a sacrifice for forgiveness of sin.

He made salvation available, but it's not automatic. A person has to reach out and call on Him in faith.

The Bible says, *"Whoever shall call upon the name of the Lord shall be saved"* (Romans 10:13). Jesus said, *"Behold, I stand at the door and knock. If you will let Me in, then I will come in"* (Revelation 3:20). It's like someone coming to your door and knocking, but if you don't open the door, they're never going to be able to come in.

I remember two weeks before my twentieth birthday. I was on my way to hell on a banana peel, but I made a commitment of my life to Christ. I called on the name of the Lord. I asked Jesus Christ to come into my heart, to forgive me of every sin, to heal me of every sickness and disease. God raised me up, and a change came into my life. That's when God's call came on my life.

It wasn't automatic. No, I had to call on the name of the Lord to be saved. We all must make that choice. And it's up to us who know Him to share this news with those who don't yet know Him.

LUKE 14:23

Then the master said to the servant, Go out into the highways and hedges, and compel them to come in, that my house may be filled.

Friend, yes, we are living in the end times. But listen to what I am going to tell you. Do not get overly preoccupied with what is going on in the world right now. Don't obsess over the news. Do not become so consumed with world events that you miss out on participating in God's plan in these last days. Don't miss out!

Now, I'm not saying that you should be ignorant to what is going on in the world. But it's time for us as Christians to give God our very best for the end-time harvest of souls. We must hold nothing back! There are souls to be won, and God will help us to bring people to

Him, if we'll trust Him to do it.

Where is the harvest field? The harvest field is wherever there are unsaved people. It's in your neighborhood, on your job, at your school, and in your family. It's in your community and your nation. And it's all over the world. The earth is ripe for harvest! It's time to get out and share the Gospel, the Good News of Jesus, with everyone we can reach.

PROVERBS 11:30

The fruit of the righteous is a tree of life, and he who wins souls is wise.

MATTHEW 4:19

Then He said to them, follow Me, and I will make you fishers of men.

If you're worried about how to win souls, don't let fear stop you. Jesus said, "I will make you fishers of men." He is the One who will empower you to do it. He'll help you! If you'll trust Him and just begin sharing Him with others, doors will open for you to reach them.

Be Ready

Perhaps you have one final question for me. "Richard, how can I know that I'm ready for the Lord's return?"

I am so glad you asked that! First, I encourage you to develop a strong relationship with the Lord in these last days. How do you do that? Find yourself a good Bible-believing church and a pastor who is highly anointed by the Holy Spirit. Be faithful to God through your local church.

Second, be a person who reads God's Word daily. Be a person of prayer. Set aside time in your daily routine to spend with the Lord.

Third, don't be surprised when the world is critical of what we believe. Jesus Himself in Matthew 24 said the world was going to hate us. We're seeing that right now. We're seeing the world take a stand against Christianity. It's the devil at work. I even saw recently where a well-known female television host said, "Anyone who says that God has spoken to them is mentally off."

When I heard that, it made me think about Mother Teresa, who said God spoke to her. Was Mother Teresa mentally off? I don't think so. Martin Luther King Jr. said that God spoke to him. Was he mentally off? I don't think so. I knew Billy Graham most of my life. Billy

Graham said that God spoke to him. Was he mentally off? I don't think so. All my life growing up as Oral Roberts' son, I heard my father say God spoke to him and told him to do various things. Was he mentally off? I don't think so.

And I have news for you. God has spoken to me many times. Am I mentally off? I don't think so. But that's how some in the world think. And we'll hear more of that kind of thinking as the world grows darker. Don't let it discourage you or make you fearful, because as a Christian, you can know without a doubt that God is with you.

Give Your Heart to the Lord

Finally, my last piece of advice to you is this:

If you have not been walking closely with the Lord, there is no better time to change that than right now! If ever there was a time to give your heart to Christ, now is the time.

All these things that the Bible has prophesied are coming to pass, and they're coming to pass very quickly. It's time to give your heart to the Lord, not out of fear but because He loves you, because He's concerned about you. He not only wants you to have a good life on this earth, but He wants you to live forever with Him.

Maybe you've never committed your life to Christ. Maybe you've never repented and turned your back on the devil and said, "I don't want the devil; I want God in my life." Or maybe you have strayed away from God and His Word, and you haven't spent time with Him in a long time. Maybe you've wandered away from His calling on your life, and you know you need to turn back, repent, and make things right between you and Him.

I believe Jesus Christ is knocking on the door to your heart right now. Remember what He said: "If you'll open the door, I will surely come in." This is the greatest love story of all. Do you want to be a part of it?

Right now is the time to give your heart to the Lord. Don't wait another day. Don't wait another hour. Don't wait another second.

Pray this prayer out loud with me, right now:

Oh, God, be merciful to me, a sinner. I admit I have sinned, Lord, and I'm sorry. I repent of my sins. I ask Jesus Christ to come into my heart to save and heal me, to deliver me and to set me free. I renounce Satan and all his works. I don't want him in my life. I receive Jesus as my Lord and Savior. Come into my heart, Lord Jesus. Fill me with Your Holy Spirit so that I may live my life for You. Amen.

Richard Roberts
P.O. Box 2187
Tulsa, OK 74102-2187

www.oralroberts.com

For prayer, call ***The Abundant Life Prayer Group*** at 918-495-7777, or contact us online at **www.oralroberts.com/prayer**.